RUNNING THE DUSK

ACKNOWLEDGMENTS

Versions of these poems have appeared in the following publications:

Calabash: "Curry Powder"; "A Dream of Fire"; *Callaloo:* "To Hold a Meditation"; "Goodman's Bay II"; *Caribbean Beat:* "Legba"; *Caribbean Review of Books:* "Goodman's Bay"; *Cave Canem Anthology:* "Groove"; *Caribbean Erotic Anthology* (Peepal Tree): "The Empress of Slackness" and "On Listening to Shabba While Reading Césaire"; *Indiana Review:* "Legba"; *Maple Tree Literary Supplement:* "Cheekbones" and "Iguana"; *MiPOesias:* "Lightskinned Id"; *New Caribbean Poetry* (Carcanet): "Goodman's Bay", "Shells for Sonia Sanchez", "Legba", "Yellow Rooms", "Groove", "On Listening to Shabba While Reading Césaire", "Rudical"; *New Poetries IV* (Carcanet): "Dover to Accra", "At Buckingham Palace", "Briland Aubade", "Rudical", "Shells for Sonia Sanchez", "Curry Powder"; *Obsidian III:* "Shells for Sonia Sanchez"; *Oxford/Cambridge May Anthologies:* "Vertigo"; *Oxonian Review:* "Moruga", "Shells for Sonia Sanchez"; *PN Review:* "Dover to Accra", "The First Time I Made Curry", "Briland Aubade"; *Sable:* "Robert Love Monument"; *Small Axe:* "Yellow Rooms", "Rudical", "What the Vibe Is"; *The Drunken Boat*: "Ballad of Oxfraud"; *Tongues of the Ocean:* "Iguana"; *Wasafiri:* "A Federation of Wings", "Ballad of Oxfraud"; *West Branch:* "Give Thanks in the Morning".

CHRISTIAN CAMPBELL

RUNNING THE DUSK

Poetry series editor: Kwame Dawes

PEEPAL TREE

First published in Great Britain in 2010
Peepal Tree Press Ltd
17 King's Avenue
Leeds LS6 1QS
UK

ISBN 13: 9781845231552

Supported by
ARTS COUNCIL
ENGLAND

Give thanks for the fellowship and grant support from Duke University, the Rhodes Trust, the University of Oxford and the Bahamas Endowment for the Performing Arts.

Give thanks for community: Four Bean Stew, the Carolina African American Writers Collective, Slice( ) Mango, the Arvon Foundation, the Fine Arts Work Center in Provincetown, the Calabash Festival and, above all, Cave Canem (CC Massive!), laboratory, movement, family.

Give thanks to so many mentors, teachers and friends for their support, critique and light in the shaping of this book: Yusef Komunyakaa, Elizabeth Alexander, Lorna Goodison, Derek Walcott, Mervyn Morris, Sonia Sanchez, Martha Rhodes, Shara McCallum, Remica Bingham, Asha Rahming, Marion Bethel, Angelique Nixon (for taking my work seriously in her important dissertation), Ian Strachan, Ishion Hutchinson, Evie Shockley, Mendi Obadike, Idara Hippolyte and Aracelis Girmay.

Give thanks to John Beadle for the magnificent cover and Erica James for her wise eyes.

Give thanks to Jeremy Poynting and Hannah Bannister for this and for all that they do for Caribbean literature.

Give thanks to Kwame Dawes (and the spirit of the late Neville Dawes) for his support, friendship and generosity of spirit.

Give thanks to my family in The Bahamas and Trinidad & Tobago and everywhere.

Give thanks to all my ancestors, dusk people.

For Daddy Mummy Carlyle

who stand in the gap

CONTENTS

The hour when street lamps are lit in the city, and which children try to drag out so that they can go on playing, though their eyes, suddenly active, are closing in spite of themselves. The hour in which – and it's a space rather than a time – every being becomes his own shadow, and thus something other than himself. The hour of metamorphoses, when people half hope, half fear that a dog will become a wolf.

Jean Genet, "Prisoner of Love"

En tu remota tierra ha caído esta luz difícil…
Pablo Neruda, "Hymno y Regreso"

All this difficult light has fallen on your lonely land…

I.

GOODMAN'S BAY

BUCKING UP ON EVENING

When the whole of the sky
is beside me, and all live things
are clearing away,

I run through the small
valleys of sand searching.

Time to time I dare
myself to race the sun
and when I think

I am in the lead,
I see my shadow ahead
pacing me step for step,

already in the blue hour,
around my shoulders
like a shawl.

Flash between wake and sleep,
sound of a proud man passing,

one turn of the body
and there it is.

How you send me
deep into forgetting –

where I am, what I want,
the name of someone I love.

A FEDERATION OF WINGS

There was no sound
but I looked out my window
anyway, through cracks

in the hedge to a cricket match,
glimpse after glimpse
of baptismal white, then away

from the whitepatched hedge
to two pigeons warring
in a fir tree, or mating,

flapping light and shadow
onto my wall. Sun already
drifting, they, two pigeons,

were making the low
light blink through
my window-aperture.

I never knew pigeons
had such beauty in them.
Because their eyes

can see far
and are orange
as the sun now trailing.

Sometimes my heart,
you see, is like a swarm
of pigeons.

Here in Oxford
the pigeons are bold,
vicious, glide like bats.

On Ship Street they swoop
down in gangs, steal
bread from tourists.

Once an old woman,
grey too, and grimy,
on a bench, was feeding

a clamour of them,
cooing in their
pigeon-talk.

She fed them
like a mother giving
seeds and milk.

The sound of pigeons,
the bouncing neck,
I sometimes hate them.

But then, it seems,
there is also
the loveliness of pigeons –

my first time in Trafalgar
Square, waiting for a visa,
I did what everyone must do –

I spread my arms
like a child and flew
into their gossip, rousing

a blizzard of beautiful ash.

GOODMAN'S BAY

A chewed bone, a used rubber
in the seaweed, cut glass
smiling beneath the sand.
We don't see them.

He is my brother.
I have bad shoulders,
he has bad knees. We have
given our bodies an atlas.

We run the dusk
at dusk. Everything
is open and live
with silence. God,
there is too much
red in the sky!

Making braille in the sand
like this, we feel it in the lower back.
The sinking, the slipping,
all the slopes and mounds.
We are listening to the body.

Whoever needs to howl
should howl. The warm breath
coming from the sea. The full moon
pulls the tide, a stubborn skirt.

Children squawk on a swing, flying,
Bahamian children in the night,
the hotels a glance away.

You feel it when you run
the sand. All of it,
the whole of your body
in the world. The swing
creaks slow, like love
in the morning. God,
the night is so blue!

Man and woman in the dark
water. Ghost and ghost on the seawall.
Someone sews false hair
into a slim girl's dreams.
She does this at night for no good reason.
All this beauty for nothing.

Walking back with our chests
blooming, I taste my sweat.
There are people dusting off
their feet as if dancing.
We pass a woman in a large,
damp T-shirt, nothing but salt.
We can't see her face,
the smile or the frown, the hard
look of judgment. But the moon
is bareback and blind, and the ground
is an altar of piss and rum, and we know
somewhere on this split tongue of stone,
someone just died, just finished
making love.

MANGROVES

Dusk, and the mangroves
of clouds, which sit low
into reverie; Chinese dragons
mating or big woman riding

chariot; clouds thicker than Whitman's
beard (all angels have afros);
beneath them the hotels, giant casuarinas
in the half-dark, sawed off

and smoking. Now I must return
from the mangroves with proud
egrets, who know so much
more than me. We must

go back now to the shore
of this new night.

GOODMAN'S BAY II

"oh friendly light
oh fresh source of light"
                    Césaire

Straight to the bush to gather cracked
bottles of beer and rum, shards of seaglass
smoothed by wind and sand. We Haitian

Bahamian descendants, Burial Society
flock, crawl through the night. Since the light
at dusk is like muslin, we lay the cold

body of this man, then, on the shore
of Goodman's Bay. How he wash here
we don't know, but the workers clearing

the beach say, *This him*. John Goodman
he name, originally Jean-Paul Delattre,
brother of Stephen Dillet, first coloured man

in Parliament. Come here on a boat
from Haiti back then, back again,
so we jewel the edges of his body

with shattered bottles, then bear him
to the foot of casuarinas in order that his born
silhouette self may freely flash and prance –

luminous shadow lifting from the sand
of this beach name after a black man.

OREGON ELEGY

for I. H.

I once told a friend, who was going
to Oregon for Christmas with his girlfriend,

he'd be the only black person there
and, in fact, if you shuffle *Oregon,*

like a seasoned minstrel, it spells *Negro*
but with an extra *O* as if to make

a groan, nearly a shout, perhaps
a moment of fright: *O Negro in Oregon!*

He died laughing and told me
that's word-lynching, and I wondered

if we could also lynch words,
string them up, sever them,

tattoo them with bullets and knives;
if we could hold a barbecue

for language swaying with the branches,
soon picked to silence by crows –

words soaked in coal oil
then set ablaze, a carnival of words

sacrificed over rivers, from bridges,
from trees, too-ripe words dangling

from branches just beyond our reach.
Like Alonzo Tucker in 1906,

shot twice, then hanged
from the Fourth Street Bridge

by two hundred men arched into one
white arm because (we wonder,

we know) a white woman said
he raped her. I want to tell my boy

blacks weren't wanted in Oregon
at first, but what do I know, I've never

set foot on Nez Perce land where
exactly one hundred years after

Tucker, he could go west to one edge
of America because he loves

his woman enough to be
the very last Negro on Earth.

DOVER TO ACCRA

I go running from my woman's house in Dover
Gardens to Dover Beach in order to keep my body
strong, as well as to reason with myself,
and take her route on the road – *left, right, left, then follow*
the curve down to the beach (keep South). This area
is bourgeois Barbados with houses not extravagant
but comfortable in their gorgeousness – crowds
of bougainvillea, croton, hibiscus, pastel houses with Spanish
roofs, hurricane shutters, large terra-cotta vases. I want
a house here, I think as I run, and suddenly
the gardens turn – a pink Italian restaurant,
two German women in bathsuits and flip-flops on the people's road,
a taxi driver posted on the corner outside of the Casuarina
Beach Club like a sentinel, at attention under his flags:
Broken Trident, Union Jack, Stars and Stripes.
Any minute now I expect to see a dreadlocks man,
and I turn the curve past stands of coconut souvenirs.

I am running this morning to Dover Beach,
not going someplace where "the cliffs of England stand."
But before I know it, Arnold gets bust in the chops,
his bushy mutton chops, by Sean Paul: *BREAKOUT BREAKOUT*
(bruk wine), BREAKOUT BREAKOUT! At last my dreadlocked
spar toting a boombox on his shoulder, more and more
whitepeople and Dover Beach is there. Running twice
through, I meet an obstacle course of umbrellas, palms
and lounge chairs cradling people as red and wrinkled
as salt prunes; they are English so they want to sunbathe
and then see their ruins. Up the surf are a few braiders and rent-
a-dreads but Bajans don't quite hustle and shuffle like us.

I am here in Dover, in Christchurch, Barbados, with my woman
who is beautiful and waiting for me, who has always waited for me.
And when I return from my run, we will spend the day at Accra

Beach. Kamau Brathwaite said, "Barbados, most English
of West Indian islands, but at the same time nearest, as the slaves fly,
to Africa." We will go from Dover to Accra with my woman's friends,
two generations of *bonda Ma Jacques* pretty Dominican women
and I will tell them all that their beaches are nothing compared
to my pink coral sand and water like blue chiffon in The Bahamas,
baja mar, shallow sea. I will go the colour of molasses mixed
with bronze, the tone of a sweet, dark rum in Accra,
and we will all swallow the sun whole on Accra
Beach, near the hotel, in Little England, Little Africa,
in love with skin on this second day of the year.

BALLAD OF OXFRAUD

I.

Bright barefoot boy from Marsh Harbour,
Abaco; Abaco that wish to remain with the Crown
when the country wanted free. Abaco
of the Conchie Joe bosses, the subtle suck-teeth
of black Bahamians and the rising tide of Haitians.
Pigeon Pea, Sand Banks, The Mud, barefoot black
boy who did want follow the footpaths of T.S. Eliot.
Green Turtle Cay, Coopers Town, No Name Cay,
Man-o-War Cay, Marsh Harbour, Cherokee Sound,
seventeen year-old boy with sharkskin tough foot-bottom
at the base of a candy-cane lighthouse reciting
"Hollow Men". Island boy who dared to apply
to Merton College, Oxford and get a turn-up nose,
but slip into Oxford Brookes Uni. nearby, good enough
to sneak a glance at Merton some days and listen
to the recording of "The Wasteland", practising
that deadpan, faux English accent.
Island colonial with good practice already.

II.

Up the road at Univ. College, poor Vidia
Naipaul, decades before, sleeping with the heat
turn all the way up, waking up in a sweat,
swamp-wet nightmare that he was back
in Trinidad. Just the other day the headline
of *The Sun* was, Would you let this man
near your daughter? Why yes, they were referring
to Benjamin Zephaniah, Rasta poet, nominated
for Oxford Professor of Poetry. T.S. Eliot
was who this rockfoot man wish to be

and since he could not, why not beat Oxford
dons at they own game? Why not flam the spires
and go back home to a country that reward
the best flam, the best sham? Why not earn
a Master's in Tingumology, an LLB
in Dis 'n Dat, a PhD in Flamology? He trod
all over Europe and America swinging whitefolk
with his black Eliot jig. He wear ascots
and bowties, long Merton College scarves
and rolled his *R's* like thunder. Everyone
at Oxford was a fraud, and he could outdon
the dons, Oxford Professor of Flam,
chickcharney of chicanery, of dupery,
bamboozlement, hoodwink, hustle, baloney;
of banana oil, Abaco hogwash, skulduggery,
swindle, fourberie, skunk, fix, shuffle, hoax.

III.

City of dreaming spires

City of beaming liars

City of screaming fires

Tweed jacket never washed

Tweed jacket never washed

P.I. Bridge is falling down

falling down falling down

Fancy dancer Junkanoo

Fancy dancer Junkanoo

IV.

Back to The Bahamas, a red carpet rolled
for him, hardfoot Abaco man, dancing
in the road for our Oxbridge don.
All the fraud had make his hair fall out, had colour
his teeth a yellow English shade, had fatten
him like a Christmas feast hog, stuffed as a straw
doll, full full of hot air, he was bald and plump
as a West Indian M.P., fat men playing God.
He wear 3-piece suits every Jesus Christ day
in Nassau bushfire heat. He fight the Anglican
priests and the lawyers that article locally
for the best Oxbridge clip and tone. His mug
grace the papers every other day, resident expert
on the economy, politics, history, philosophy and,
most importantly, Dis 'n Dat.

SIDNEY POITIER STUDIES

UNIVERSITY OF CAMBRIDGE INTERNATIONAL EXAMINATIONS
General Certificate in Education
Ordinary Level Studies

Section A (100 Marks)

Choose the option that best describes Sir Sidney Poitier.
Poitier is _____ :

(a) A barefoot Bahamian boy of so-they-say Haitian
blood who grow up pickin tomato on Cat Island.

(b) The perfect black man and the rightful heir
to the Kingdom of Negrolandia.

(c) The G.O.A.T. (Greatest Of All Time).

(d) A Civil Rights cyborg invented by MLK,
X, Garvey and black genius scientists.

(e) A Victorian rebel.

(f) Chuckling at his image on the screen,
sprawled on the couch, his shirt fully unbuttoned.

(g) All of the above.

LEGBA

A well-loved lit classic
packed in each bag, and a Harvard
sweatshirt to match the Pakistani
passport – Iqbal goes first, catching
a flight to France. Then me,
in a tie and soft pants, khaki hat
to keep my head tame. We chat
clipped and colonial, like our tutors,
grinning out *Oxford* with a nod.
At immigration I put on airs
and styles, let the maleness growl
without teeth. Hold my chest
with untouchable height. All like
a politician, a Sidney Poitier,
an old Bahamian man. I look
only ahead and walk straight-back,
like my grandfather. Speak like he spoke
to foreigners. In his best moods,
he would put on the mouths
of all the Englishmen he'd met,
playing the Queen and how
she gave him his MBE – Pa.
There, reciting and reciting Blake,
until he fell down blank and silent
as any road in Nassau
the morning after junkanoo.

TO HOLD A MEDITATION

And then I dive, serene as a turtle,
goggles strapped tight; I am the bronze-haired
men at Arawak Cay who dive for conch
all day. I am looking for shells
and pebbles, bits of coral, to turn over

and over in my hands, but half-hidden
by the blue-brown reef is a body tombed
in amber and seaweed. It is
my grandfather, brought back now by dayclean
tide (having set his body to sea since time).

Laid out on the shore, he is a shell of the sea's
patience. Still in his blind-white
catechist's gown, now all laced with seaweed,
coral has cocooned his legs, caked
his greying hair. Eyes closed with two stones.

All on shore rejoice my find – the brethren,
the braiders, the cigar sellers, the lovers.
We smoke spliffs from pages of the Bible:
first Peter, then Matthew, then all of Psalms.
We crouch under casuarinas (praise

these trees older than anything
we know). We hold a meditation.

LISTENING TO THE BODY

I.

I pierced my ear at fourteen,
the left one, at the mall, a hole
in it, being pretty like that –
smooth, a sting, a new self.

Having a hole and you could be
seen on the inside – stud through slit,
snapped to back, shining.
Swabbing the raw place, rubbing it,
slipping the gold through my ear,
I tilted my head to the side like a woman
in the mirror.

But now it is not, closed up,
flesh in flesh,
keloid on the lobe,
painless ball, plaything, bubby,
my third nipple.

II.

My aunt bathes him.
She knows the body.
He has fluid racing through
a tube like a river.
He lays there.
His penis dumb and covered,
sheath to tube to piss-bag.

His left side dead,
you can feel the man bone-deep.
What do I know? What do I know?

Calf muscles soft as a lobe.
Today even a lizard won't watch,
so still, so still on the wall.

"GIVE THANKS IN THE MORNING"

— Beres Hammond

The workmen sing to themselves
in the morning
at Potter's Cay Dock,

unload boxes of fruit and fish
off the mailboat at dayclean
and sing, hair all bronzed,
cut throughout like marble.

All morning pumping
iron like Adonis,
I come home
sweaty and electric to sing
and look at how muscle
is like a rose.

The body is broad and lean
with long limbs, a swimmer shape,
Yoruba and hungry
to become barrel-chested,
the hull of a ship.

Running the Paradise Island
Bridge one morning, I heard the workmen
singing but I did not understand.

My grandfather sang broadvoice and coarse,
harmonising in the oldpeople way.
He beat the sun to waking every day
he was alive, to read the Bible
and pray for his children.
He sold tomatoes to Miami
to send his children to school.

Not even my woman
can hear me singing now
as I bathe and make a map
on the body with cocoa butter,
smooth my mane with coconut oil.

Bareskin in the morning,
I want everything
but to stop the jubilee;

a song to wash the day,
O Jah, to bless
my waking clean.

AT BUCKINGHAM PALACE

I

I am the first of my family
to go to Buckingham Palace.
I had the flu, I nearly stayed home;
left my hair in all its might,
wore a beige linen suit.

Her Majesty was in a red dress
with horrid black gloves,
her hair like rigor mortis.
This was not the White House.
She was very, very calm.

Van Dyck, Rubens,
Rembrandt, Canaletto
from all angles, oil paintings
on the ceilings and walls. The eyes
of Anglo nobles glaring down,
draperies, mirrors and all.
Sèvres porcelain, Canova
and Chantrey sculpture,
servants, secret rooms,
French furniture.
But no crown jewels
from India in sight,
none from Benin.

Mister, Mister,
where have you been?
I been to London
to see the Queen.

Some of the ladies curtsied,
some of the men bowed.
The Queen raised her black glove
high (as with rings and bent wrists)
and I received the Royal Chalice:

Light up your spliff,
Light up your chalice,
Make we smoke it inna
Buk In Hamm Palace.

II

The Queen came to Nassau
when I was eight.
The whole family walked
to streets lined like Boxing Day,
to see her pass in a green Jaguar,
to see that white-gloved wave
borrowed in pageants, float parades.

Benjamin Zephaniah, Rasta poet,
turned down the OBE. *Up yours,*
he said, *No way Mr. Blair, no way Mrs. Queen.*
When my grandfather got that MBE,
name blazing on the Queen's
New Year's Honours List,
Her Majesty told him something
that he would stage for guests
for years, displaying his medal
as a child shows a good wound.
Wear your best suit, he would have said,
Make sure cut your hair, shine up
your shoes.

CURRY POWDER

Panday in power now, somebody cries.
They think they better than people,
my Trini cousins say, *And they like*
wear Fila shoe. My brother and I
laugh and add, *They is smell strong*
like curry powder. Is true, we say.

Coolies and niggers fighting these days
but great-grandmummy Nita did not fight
when she found herself facing the West
instead, touching the face of a Grenadian,
Manny. She did not wear saris no more.
Calypso she liked and could wine down
with the best of them. She became deaf
to the melody of *Krishna's* flute.
She chose Manny, not *Lord Rama* in her
Hindu epic gone wrong. At her wedding
she never once uttered *Ganesh's* name,
loosened the grasp of *Vishnu's*
four hands from round her waist.
Her sisters disowned her in the holy
name of Mother India. But she made
dougla babies anyway and did not give
them the sacred names of gods: *Brahma,*
Shiva, Gauri. She named Grandaddy
Leon, a good European name, like all the other
rootless Negroes.

You know how people go, it took many deaths
and many births for the Mullchansinghs to talk
to the Brathwaites again and, finally, Mummy
and her siblings were born looking Indian enough.
But Panday in power now and Mummy warned
me to say *Indian* not *coolie.* One of my small

36

cousins told me, with a grown-up intuition, *You know,*
in Trinidad, you not black, you dougla.

Panday in power now and my cousins still cuss
about neighbours with jhandi flags of many colours
claiming their yards for as many gods as there are
colours, after which we all go to eating pelau
with roti and curry, leaving our fingers stained
yellow like old papers so we, too, stink
of curry powder.

CHEEKBONES

When my Bahamian grandfather passed,
my uncle asked for a Madeira coffin
that would set them off.

Another uncle, the eldest on my Trinidadian side,
explained that they, twin boulders, were the reasons
shopkeepers in Brooklyn spoke to him in Spanish.

Long ago my grandmother, Carib Queen, turned through
the soil in Moruga, and handed me these two moons.

Then she walked back to Venezuela,
rising out a mountain, a blaze.

IGUANA

for A.T.

My friend from Guyana
was asked in Philadelphia
if she was from "Iguana."

Iguana, which crawls and then
stills, which flicks its tongue at the sun.

In History we learned that Lucayans
ate iguana, that Caribs
(my grandmother's people)
ate Lucayans (the people of Guanahani).
Guiana (the colonial way,
with an *i*, southernmost
of the Caribbean) is iguana; Inagua
(southernmost of The Bahamas,
northernmost of the Caribbean)
is iguana – Inagua, crossroads with Haiti,
Inagua of the salt and flamingos.
The Spanish called it *Heneagua*,
"water is to be found there,"
water, water everywhere.

Guyana (in the language of Arawaks,
Wai Ana, "Land of Many Waters")
is iguana, veins running through land,
grooves between green scales.
My grandmother from Moruga
(southernmost in Trinidad)
knew the names of things.
She rubbed iguana with bird pepper,
she cooked its sweet meat.

The earth is on the back
of an ageless iguana.

We are all from the Land of Iguana,
Hewanorra, Carib name for St. Lucia.

And all the iguanas scurry away from me.
And all the iguanas are dying.

II.

MASQUERADE

LIGHTSKINNED ID

for Neruda, for The South

It so happens my id is red.
Check the clues – my lightskinned
parts: underneath my underwear,
if you pull the skin taut; on the white
hand side and down my wrist
where the veins branch out
like green pipes; my foot-bottom
and almost my eyes up close. It used
to be my whole self, until I was
six for sure. But a brownness
took over. Started swimming
at nine, how sun and chlorine
kissed the night into my skin.
There was no turning back.

But my id is good
and redboned. Like slicing open
a pear for the surprise
of its flesh. Look hard:
there's a murmur of bronze
in my skin. I'm a peanut-butter oreo,
an apple dipped in molasses;
I'm a broad dish of crème brûlée.
O the chiaroscuro of my self.

Still not freed from Freud, I'm fried
on the outside. What a brown on me!
Since the colour beneath my colour
is curried. It wants to come out,
my high yellow id. Always on the verge
of beige. It wants me to Ambi my skin,
to blossom peach all over. My id has such
a need. Here it goes with its libido of gold,

43

clashing with the ego, my I, a browner negro,
and the superego, who's a radiant absence
of white. He thinks he's in charge.

It makes me act like I'm
better than people, my id. It wants
what it wants. It makes me lick
melted margarine and steal copper
coins from bums. Makes me
bathe in mango juice. Pour sour
milk down my ears and sign
cheques in blood to prove it.
On the forms I fill in
Other and scribble *Yellow*
on the inside in red ink.
I suck the nectar beneath my skin.

My id's pretty niggerish
(for a mulatto). My id is everyone's
Indian uncle. It's taking me
to Hollywood on an undersong
of cream. My id is colourstruck
with itself. My id is El DeBarge.
My id; its job is to keep it light.
How my id misses the eighties.

If only this amber
at heart were enough.

I have to praise it. I have to lull it
with new roses. Run my fingers
along this sallow river
of desire. Stuck in the plantation
kitchen, black ants dying
in an orgy of honey.

MASQUERADE

I. Ceremonial Delivery of the Last Canes
(The King and Queen are Crowned)

In the midst of autumn's red-brick charade,
the gifts that this Boston season brings,
like the final tones of Antillean days,
is clear how colour can mark the passing

down of an empire. In Harvard Square
you catch the Leading Man and then frolic
your way to Hollywood feign. You fare
well as the English heiress: likeable, slick,

of course not the prettiest girl on screen.
Good Brit actress in American films,
end of story. But things ever as they scheme.
You would teach me to go out on a whim.

I learn to take people on place value,
though face value just as much in what's true.

II. Bridgetown Market

My conscious friends gave me the hearsee:
on that late-night show that interviews stars,
it was the bald-head host who bust your scene.
So you're from Barbados? He caught you off-garb.

Not the Mother Country, but a daughter,
this Little England. Caught in the almost
where you must ever give alms. The black water
break and join who you is and how you pose.

45

Is true, is there you born, from where my great-
grandfather come. You could be a cousin.
You, too, from limestone, from cane, your first fate
in faithful sea, under unyielding sun.

But the past is more than passing fancy,
so worry, cousin, you're secret's scathed with me.

III. Cohobblopot

Just two choices for those like you who play
the foil: either marry your cousin for
dilution or flee up North where there's no day-
bloom sun to tell the truth. So it was North

that the girl-you flew, and not East like those
before you. Went for England's colonial
gloom, I assume, but you know how flying goes;
it's claimed from a thing older than the Rule

Britannia. You train to be an actress
since so-high, learn the Queen script back to front.
But where you think you learn to play mask
in the first place, to crop over the brunt

of History? Ironic that you take
great-granddaddy own tricks to flee his face.

IV. Calypso Monarch

Trust me, I should have known all along.
I get it now: your wide mouth, your hair, a screen
of spiralled question marks, features nearly strong,
almost heavy, all the metaphors that mean

a people. Would Heartthrob still go hunting
for you if he knew? Maybe I don't blame you.
Dared to ape the Queen to be Master or win
Mistress, to miss the stress of red cane you grew.

Who say Bajans can't be beige as the shore?
Sure, on the cover of Cosmo you came out
tanned and freckled as family, obscure
no more. Cousin, you must be more devout

to pass the test. You must stay in character,
play the mass, to be Queen of Crop Over.

V. Grand Kadooment

Could be a chameleon in the parade
but that metaphor would be too easy.
Name so odd, I'd risk getting punish; trade
place and time, and you'd have been Miss Daisy

driver, not the star, but the supporting
cast of History's Mini-drama. You,
nearly as deceptive as puns, trying
to Eshú time and face. Not many know

how well you dance. I, too, make mas at the Grand
Kadooment; I smile for the chimera.

This sun plays tricks and sugar sends you mad.
Do you see my colours, my dazzling terror?

Watch my style, my chalkface charade, rude
work harvesting hymns. Break way. Look good.

YELLOW ROOMS

In Grenada, my woman island, for the first time
without her, at my writer-friend place
in Morne Jaloux, verandah view

out to bush bush bush
then the Carenage,
we were liming in the kitchen

talking good talk bout books
and freshness over oil-down
cook up by her boxer-boyfriend

when, just so, a bat fly in the place,
winging wild, nearly buck up
the walls. Everybody duck,

scream with a kind of delight.
It fly fly fly like a madness,
like moth on fire.

The radar off, my friend say.
The damn thing couldn't find
the door it fly in from.

Is a fruit bat right?
I laugh a tremble-laugh.
This creature just come

and mash up all the vibes,
all blind, hairy, all blur.
Even love, I learn, could be just so,

not meant for this house,
these small, yellow rooms,
a notion, a so-and-so,

old suckblood idea;
who say it could fly in,
dance up in the air and thing?

Not a window open again
to chase the thing back out.
Come in like it want stay

for true,
come cause commotion
in I heart.

THE FIRST TIME I MADE CURRY

You left your scrunchee here that last time.
On the dresser, there forgetting your scent.
You only wore it when you smoked (slim, mint
Nat Shermans), to spare your hair. The first time
I made curry, there was smoke. Six whole nights
it stained the air – a thing in my kitchen
alive. I think you were gone by then.
But it was good, plenty channa, not too mild.

I stopped cutting my hair again, just in
time for the cold. Haven't met any other
West Indians yet. I don't have time to miss
a beat. Every dayclean I still swim –
like nothing. Like every Friday, Next Door
must still cuss out her married man and fry fish.

THE EMPRESS OF SLACKNESS
for Lady Saw

Parting your legs
like wings, flying,

even strobe lights
cannot catch your skin.

The light in which we bathe
is blue scintilla, lightning,

makes us monstrous
and divine. Selector pullup –

one thousand gaulins
flap off in fright.

Nothing but murder,
nothing but murder,

Spragga & Saw
in their tug o' war,

Nuh want nuh belly rub a dub...
Gunshot & hollers storm out.

Madness now. Melody
like a tripped alarm,

like an ambulance
come for those who can't

handle the ride. All woman
hands on knees, rolling, pumping,

churning; one grand factory
of flesh. Your black

belly ripples. Fool your body
into being a snake, a hurricane,

a bull. *Right ya now Mr. Spragga*
come shot mi wid yu nine.

I swoop down on you
like a thief in a market,

start my work.
Carry on rugged, merciless,

shame the generations.
Spontaneous combustion,

middle shock out.
Pure contortion, woman,

skin out. Bust a slow
wine, a makebaby wine.

Valedictorian of the bubbling
college, you trade knowledge

with my waist. Touching
the floor, reasoning

with the underworld,
all shortskirts talking tonight.

Spooning right,
curve into groove,

we are packed like this.
Feel mi rhythm a go round

inna yu slow like di bug.
To wind is to ask questions

with your waist: Who holds
the victory? You? Me?

Snake-charmer selector?
A blackbird in leather

leads a tourist to VIP.
Two Cuban mangos on the floor,

working, shaking their gold curls,
African curves. The disco ball,

silver orb, centre,
planet spinning

all on our shadows
like an anointing.

Catwalking the aching light
we flex unstoppable.

Jungless, show me
what it means

to ride the riddim.
Slackness is an edge,

your flint tongue,
a blue hole, and we

are falling gone.
Wrecked in this well

of sound, the whole place
rocks with the sea.

Everything is a dance now:
weather and madness, animals,

transportation, chores, the works.
But what we want is backshot,

is cool and deadly.
Blame the sublime,

up against the red wall,
in this dungeon,

up against you.
Parting your legs

like gills, breathing hard,
they call this place *Fluid*

for the boneless bodies
& the gold liquor flooding;

we swim in the sound,
we drown.

VERTIGO

for Gwendolyn Brooks and Kiah

A little girl twirls in the airport,
in the line for New York. She looks
like five and already cocks out her chest.
She is adorned with womanish things,
pink plastic bangles and ruffled socks.
She opens and closes her denim jacket
like wings, as she whirls. She will come
back with more pink things (with which
to twirl). Her lips are pursed big-woman
style (she has the kind of top lip with nerve
enough to curve over the bottom one). She is
the colour of coconut candy. Her face
slopes slightly. Her cheeks are full.
Her eyes wear the seriousness
of sun. She answers to her name
and also to Precious. Her name
might be Precious. She does not fear
her smallness. She likes her Bajan
ways. The spinning is all that counts.
She is already not soft and her forehead
is broad and African. If twirling and
smiling went together, she would give
one wide with dimples and her tongue
between her teeth. Singing goes with
twirling and this requires fierceness.
She knows how to hold on to the beauty
of a thing. She acts this way. You'd want
to say "she is a wailing dervish"
or "she is a rainstorm collecting".
You'd want to say "her hair is sectioned
like the parishes" or "look at Oya's
grandchild." But she is just twirling,
which her singing tells and tells. It is just that.

Her plaits are countless today, full
of bluebird barrettes. All else are staring,
sensible and still. The girl gives a whirl.

SHELLS

for Sonia Sanchez and Kerha

You ten, I six, and jujube
now in season. I monkey up
the tree and call down
to you, not Wilsonia, that
big-people name. I does call you
Nita. Only them small ocean eyes
say how you know, I know,
my Mummy know that, boy, jujube
stain don't come out. I'll do most
anything for these plump little suns
and you, even with wasps telling
secret. Is breaktime still and your legs
look skinny under that plaid skirt. You is
give me quarters sometimes, to buy salty.
You's always have your hair in one,
rake and scrape to the side, and if
that don't mean womanish, I don't know
what does. You's the one that start everyone
saying, *That's my prerogative!* You stink
to them teachers but not one child at Xavier's
could test you at singing. I tell people
you's my cousin, but you really the one
that I lend my recorder to longtime
so you wouldn't get licks
and you did never forget it.

One time you tell me Santa Claus
fake cause we don't have no chimney
in Nassau and his skin too pink
for this kinda sun and I was sad
because I was hoping for one new bike
so you let me go first in handball.
We always have to pray every assembly

58

Our father who art in heaven
Harold be thy name and I ask you
why Harold so mean to never show
me his art? And the grin how you
answer is keep me glad for days.
I most tall as you, you know, but you
could beat me and plenty boys running
any day, quick as a curly-tail lizard.
Sometimes, when I feel like it, I go up
to people in the schoolyard and point
and say, *What you name?* and you laugh
big as America.

The children don't like me cause
I know my numbers and hard words too
and you say is cause they still is
pee the bed. The children say you
don't have no Mummy and your mouth
too hot. That mouth. Like two piece
of pepper, it stay poke out, look like
it shape for cussing. Turkey neck, pointer
finger, tripping on your tongue. My
Miss Biggety, with your little red self.
Yes you. You who is hum for the trees
always and play ringplay and pinch
the boys that get too fresh. If I did know
you was going with your Daddy to leave
me for true, I would of give you all
my shells and soldier crabs, and even my
new chain. I would of make you learn me
to run fast and sing, if I did know New York
was far-far like the moon.

BRILAND AUBADE

after Lorna Goodison

Roosters flounce around
like Lord Dunmore must have done,
broad-chested and pompous,

brilliantly plumed. They have broken
their pact with the Briland sun.
Too aloof for a dayclean crow,

they let the island sleep in,
call out when they please.
Briland only big enough

for golf carts to sput through
archways draped with bougainvillea,
red crown canopy

for a bride and groom, through
rock roads of cocoa plum bush,
sea grape, dark blushing croton.

Never pass an old woman
on her clapboard porch
without saying *Mornin*.

At the Pink Sands beach
we descend into peace breeze
and the sea rising like a staircase

of lapis lazuli, blues live
beyond belief. If Winslow Homer
painted this place, he'd paint

small boys barking coconut
on the postcard shore
without eyes or mouths. But could he

catch the faint faint rose of the sand,
as if tinged by blood from a beach
massacre two hundred years ago?

Fish-belly models crane
and arch for a photoshoot
near pastel cottages.

Expats and winter residents lounge
in these twinned tropics
of Africa and New England,

in this wooden, white-fenced
commonwealth of skyjuice
and colonial slumber.

White Brilanders birthday their homes,
three hundred years of family
ground: Loyalists, Adventurers

from Bermuda, Preacher's Cave-dwellers,
seekers of *Eleutheria* — Greek
for freedom, slavery,

apprenticeship, prohibition,
rum-running. Old Bahamian
prejudice. But the sea

forgives it all. Dunmore Town
hums with youths in psychedelic
Oakley shades, twine-up hair;

they run the rentals, prowl the docks
for prey as the young girls grow
ripe on Miami dreams.

What else is there to do
on an island big as a stone?
Drift like a tourist through

Colebrooke St. and Dunmore St.,
through *Eva's Straw Work* and *Dunmore
School*, *The Landing*, *Starfish Restaurant*,

Nappy's for the best gourmet pizza
and cracked conch, Ma Ruby's dinner
at *Tingum Village Hotel*, *Wesley Methodist

Church*, *Avery's* for a boil fish breakfast,
Seagrapes Club, *Vic-hum's Lounge*,
under the stars, best club on Briland.

Once you have touched
this Harbour Island, you are bound
to come back. We sing

I got sand in my shoe,
quadrille to rake 'n scrape
like the old people. Dunmore Town

is older than America
and we are two Nassau folks
seeking sea-song and romance.

At Romora Bay, I wake to silence,
to the sun pressed against the
mauve curtain, its morning veil.

I wake to you standing
naked in the mirror.
You are combing your hair.

A DREAM OF FIRE

I.

It start like a dark calypso:
Man think Woman scheming on Man.
Man spit gasoline on Woman
and fling a match.
Woman run and everything done.

To light match in a straw market,
most things catch: straw dolls, *Hey Mon*
T-shirts, African statues made in Japan,
daishikis, trinkets, straw hats, Androsia
dresses, knock-off Gucci bags, floral sarongs,
the cries of *Prettygirl* and Walcott poems.

The braiders would spider
hair and recite "The Schooner *Flight*"
for $20, one bead per line.
But now the people are laughing
or crying and all we see is one red man
running out of the blaze. Out of the fire
bust open like dawn.

These heavy women with huge hands,
hats, and long skirts, these straw vendors,
would plait straw tighter than sonnets and hustle
Walcott poems on the side. In the dream
they shake their grey-heads at the howl
of fire. A bird, a sea-swift, might think
it Soufrière. But it's just a burning market.

II.

Walcott is safe, thank God, no longer
limps. Poems gone, poems gone.
But he knows them all by heart,
like the braiders. Poems gone,
he sucks his teeth and grumbles:
History. First time in Nassau,
last stop on the schooner *Flight*,
he paints the market skanking down
in flames, cigarette painting smoke,
too, from his mouth.

He paints one of the braiders
knitting my hair, diamond style:
Open the map. More islands there, man,
than peas on a tin plate, all different size,
one thousand in the Bahamas alone...
A big-belly man is making
fritters to sell, so I don't smell
poems burning. Only oil, batter,
bubbling conch.

Smoke barrels up like music.
The singed straw dolls lip-synch
Arrow: *Olé Olé, Olé Olé...*
and ya room-boom-boom-boom
(and for once the old man dance).

Bay Street burns like the sixties, like 1942.
Funky Nassau. There is no place like this.
Armagiddeon or obeah, only us.
Everyone knows what we like:
we like pretty. So what matters in the dream,
the scrap gangs running to catch ashes
for new costumes and how beautiful
Bay Street will look
with a whole other mouth.

GROOVE

– In the other voice of Winston Shakespeare,
How Stella Got Her Groove Back

I never born.
I walk out the water one day,
gleaming and black.
I walk out the water one day,
between Atlantis and The Shack.

Me, I come from conch-songs
and fire and under limbo bars,
wooden monkeys in barrels
where huge dicks spring out,
clapboard houses, goombay,
a raggamuffin's bop, the Ministry
of Tourism. My thing, my thing.

I make of muscle
and rum and straw;
tiny umbrellas and beads;
and the Bible and Shakespeare
and Africa.

I use to have bubbies,
ripe and handy. I was
a Marketwoman. I was
a Banana Man. I use
to do the fire dance.
I use to run the glass-
bottom boat. I use to rent jet skis
in the kingdom of this beach.

I could fuck
like a goatskin drum.
But the braiders thief my lyrics:
Prettygirl Prettygirl Prettygirl.
I could fuck like a drum.

All day I lift plenty
legs. I prowl. I ride.

Somebody pounce a white gyal,
leave her in the bush to dead.

I lift plenty legs. I prowl. I ride.

The black ones believe we
family, but I don't know
them niggers from Adam.

These hotels like mountains.
You have to be barefoot.
You have to dance.
You have to have chest.
When my locks start to sprout,
I will make double.

O I have too much
to want.

Yes, America.
I run the islands. You come.
Look for me.

ON LISTENING TO SHABBA WHILE READING CÉSAIRE

for C.C. and C.G.

& all the purple like skin like bruise like grape like love
& all the bones get crack and the gold nipples lick
& all the kinky pubic hair and fantastic abs
& all the laughter skank away with a necklace of skulls

I RISE YOU UP

language like embattled iguanas
language like the nectar-crying wound

I walk on hot coals   sweet burning
lianas tremble like the body
melody sliced rectum to throat
the wind makes the sea ejaculate   & again
an old man sucks the moon's fish-eye

there in the crease crevice curve
tongues knifing names on my forearm
I eat out the sap between words

volcano of ganja   bile in the gums   spasm of blood
on Saturn's rings crotch to bottom sliding
& the two mouths together the rugged heart the juice

I would like to say:

fuckery   funk   penumbra

watermelon   biggety   viscera

anaphora	*talawa*	*slack*
orgy	*Ogun*	*guerilla*
swagger	*rum*	*flesh*

& let me say:

cerebral	*glammity*	*niggerish*
luminous	*numinous*	*stamina*
arsonist	*backshot*	*agony*
synapse	*maroon*	*gallop*
torrent	*wail*	*rudical*

I would like to say:

. . . . . .

& then:

Don of Guinea   of Gehenna
Gun of golden teeth
O do your junglist science

ROBERT LOVE MONUMENT
1835-1914

Come back Africa Abyssinia Guinea.
Ithiopia mighty nation come back.
Satta amassagana, psalm sixty-eight,
Black Star Line, Repatriation, UNIA.

The *SS Frederick Douglass*, Kingston, Harlem,
Jamaica Advocate, Emperor Selassie,
Nyabingi drums, Nyabingi drums.

Garvey, DuBois, Blyden, Padmore,
Césaire, Lumumba, Williams,
Nkrumah, Kenyatta, Senghor.

No one remember old Robert Love.
No one remember old Robert Love.

Respect due to this Bahamian man.
Gone to Jamaica, start bushfire,
teach Garvey what he know.

He who knew white minority rule,
knew a thousand islands,
mountains undersea.
Robe him in red black green.

Burning Spear, come chant a next one.

Wicked Babylon system,
all they do is lie and thief,
will not teach the children.
Bless up the man who clear
the road to Zion. He say:

Own your own land,
look to the East,
lift up the race.

Children, this a livication for Love.
Undivided everliving,
this Godbless lion.

Redemption coming, redemption coming,
the half that has never been told.
Lucaya arise and go to the harbour.
Greet your ship, your ship
of black and gold.

DONNY HATHAWAY
1945-1979
listening to "He Ain't Heavy, He's My Brother"

Lingering at the edge
of want, grasping how,
clawing, gripping again,
then leaping, spread-winged,
shape of wail, taking yes
to good night. Rivering,
ghosting in a slow-drag:
churching gravity. Praise
armed to hold bones, larynx
of soldered gold, soldier
for the blues coup, heaven
flung, for what's coursing out.
Past the plunge of need, of we,
when salt-throat bears all
to the blood of undone.

RUDICAL

Derek Bennett, killed by the police

after Matisse's Icare (Jazz), 1943

I who born
Twenty-four years
Since *The Windrush* come
Twenty-four years
Life of a man
I who born
Four gold bullets
Life of a man
I who born

    & because we suck the neon of the streets
    & because we tote a solar plexus of islands (*it's true*)
    & because we yuck out the blue heart of night (*right*)
    & because our heads gather thick as a bloodclot (*teach them*)
    & because we eat out the honey of mad laughter (*everytime*)
    & because we outrun the delirium of streetlights (*more fire*)
    & because we are bugs scuttling from the lifted rock
    & because & because & &
    & because each eyehole grows iridescent with the moon
    & because we holler for the bloodclad sun
    & because we mourn the burst testes of the stars
    & because we skank cross rivers of blood

Mine New Cross mine Oldham Notting Hill Bradford Brixton mine
too Nassau Laventille Bridgetown Kingston Britain has branded an
x this rolled throat of killings this septic eye of maggotry this seed of
Mars this blasted plot this hurt realm this ogly island this England

PARDON I SOLDIER

for Carlyle

Is what he say
when he wanted to pass
by me and trod deeper
into the Fish Fry crowd,
jam-up, jam-up,
woman galore.

Pardon I Soldier

Is what he say
when he tap my arm
with the back of he hand,
this dread with plaits
like mine.

Pardon I Soldier

People smell green,
like a room after sex.
Conch fritters, spill
Guinness, skyjuice,
herb, piss, smoke.

Pardon I Soldier

All sweet trouble
and sound, a redjeans,
a polka-dot skirt,
a screwface and a laugh.

Pardon I Soldier

But he pass, cool rebel,
no clash, no clash.
Then gone, clean
of that moment,
whole body cocked
to the side.

Pardon I Soldier

And I prowl too,
past *Goldie's* and *Big Ten*
and *Twin Brothers*,
nodding my head
to Elephant Man,
still looking for woman.

Pardon I Soldier

Yeah, Prowler.
Don't watch nuttin.

Honourebel.
Yes, King.

A headnod,
a hand to the heart,
whatever's clever.

My Lord.
So I say the same to you:

Pardon I Soldier.
No need to fuss nor fight.

OLD MAN CHANT

To Mr. Romeo Farrington, veteran
limo driver, who appeared in a red
shortsleeve serge suit with white shoes,
praise. To the head server at *Twin
Brothers* in silver and lilac polyester,
praise. To the snow-beard man
two pews behind me in cream coat,
cream hat, cream shoes, praise.
To you grandfathers and your stingy
brims, your tie-clips and your canes, your
coloured hankies, your thick black belts
and your blazing wingtips. To the sweat
you rain down in the name of chest-out
and swag. To you Guru Dandies,
old heads with limps and ailments,
casuarina faces. To the Black Colonial
Bush Jackets of Ministers and Doctors.

You are men named Harlington,
Errol, Clive, Israel, Theophilus,
Cleveland, Allardyce. You are
black men named Pompey,
Solomon, Ezekiel, Napoleon,
Augustus, Elijah. You men
of two-initials-and-a-last-name
nobility. You men who went
to the *Cat 'n Fiddle* after church.
You men who smell of rum
and tiger balm, sometimes Limacol
and the musky smell of Old Spice.
You men of trembling hands
and missing teeth, sugared, sallow eyes.

You men from Cat Island
and Crooked Island and Andros
and Long Island and Inagua
and Abaco and all. You men
who walked to the Panama
Canal, to the Project in Florida,
and walked the long way back.
You men with perpendicular
backs now bending. You men
who were born barefoot
but earned your shoes.
You men who still look
me straight in the eyes,
even from the Thursday
Obits. You Biblical men
with too many children. You
men who loved women
as much as you beat them.

You men of faintly British
accents in the presence of good
company. You men who could
not enter the Savoy Theatre,
walking around always alone.
You men of so many secrets,
kept names and stories, borne ache.

To you men who learned
to wear out the world,
I wave the hands of praise.

WHAT THE VIBE IS

I will have to say, *Like water*.

When I do what I want to do.

People come running
but I tell them, *Leave me, man*,
and go back to checking my pulse.

In the mirror sometimes.
My mouth. On the bridge
of the song I see the arch.

I like the mouth as I like the body.
Sweating. I like it when you can see
only teeth and eye-whites and then
smell. Every night the same dread
holds a light to the eye
of the Baygon can, soon
a dragon laughing. *More fire!*

There's some need
to kill most things.

I love the gyres of my rage,
as well as my rising chest.

So I say, *Everything cool*,
and dream of prowling past
in my ride with the diamond
rims and the beautiful system
inside.

Sooner or later I'll walk
through Bay St. dressed

as a naked man with a thick
gold chain.

Seeing as I am on the verge of cussing
out the beaches and the sun.

I wish that I could say, *Aint nothing*.
I wish I was the one who tongued
the Queen Victoria Statue with red paint.

And so?
In the growl of the morning,
I want to tell myself, *Take time*.

All I want. I want to hold
my right arm as high as I can,
the left hand holding my head.

And so? Then I think I could be
Marley's son. Bad like that.
A girl once told me,
You look like a lion. Spilled out
of his neck like Athena.

Maybe Bob came and sang in '73,
for Independence Morning, below the cannons
watching the sea. Singing us into skin,
a song never recorded, called "Grounation".

Bob had countries of sons, I know that.
We live to ride his ache like thunder.

O when "Zimbabwe" will play
in my dreams. Jah know.

And so? As for me, my great, lovely mouth
is shaped like water.

NOTES

p. 16. "Goodman's Bay II": The poem is written with thanks to my cousin Dr. Gail Saunders for sharing the history of Goodman's Bay, and Jackson Burnside for sharing the story of "moonshine baby" (also called "moonshine dolly"), a traditional game played by children in the Caribbean and West Africa. One person is chosen to be the "baby" and lies on the ground as the others in the group outline their body with materials, usually iridescent objects like shiny stones and bits of glass. When the person gets up, there is a "silhouette" on the ground and the moonshine baby is born.

p. 22. "Dover to Accra": The quote "the cliffs of England stand" is from the poem "Dover Beach" by Matthew Arnold. The italicised lines in the second stanza are from the song "Breakout" by Sean Paul.

p. 29. "To Hold a Meditation": In Rastafarian culture, the phrase "hold a meditation" means to smoke marijuana, a form of worship and meditation for Rastas.

p. 34. "At Buckingham Palace": The italicised lines in the fifth stanza are from the song "Buk-in-Hamm Palace" by Peter Tosh.

p. 52. "The Empress of Slackness": The italicised lines are from the song "Backshot" by Lady Saw and Spragga Benz.

p. 60. "Briland Aubade": The italicised phrase, *I've got sand in my shoes*, is from the song "Briland Sweet" by The Brilanders.

p. 64. "A Dream of Fire": The quote in the sixth stanza is from the poem "The Schooner *Flight*" by Derek Walcott and the quote in the seventh stanza is from the song "Hot, Hot, Hot" by Arrow.

p. 72. "Donny Hathaway": In 1979, the legendary soul singer Donny Hathaway allegedly committed suicide by jumping from the 15th floor of New York's Essex House Hotel.

p. 73. "Rudical": On July 16, 2001, Derek Bennett was shot dead by police in Brixton, South London, after brandishing a gun-shaped lighter. On July 20, 2001, a peaceful demonstration over Bennett's killing in Brixton escalated into a riot. On December 15, 2004, an inquest returned the verdict that Bennett, a twenty-nine year old black man, had been "lawfully killed." An appeal upheld this decision.

ABOUT THE AUTHOR

Christian Campbell is a writer of Bahamian and Trinidadian heritage. He studied at Macalester College in Minnesota, the University of Oxford (Balliol College) where he was a Rhodes Scholar and Duke University where he received a PhD. His poetry and essays have been published widely in journals and anthologies such as *Callaloo, Indiana Review, Small Axe, West Branch, Wasafiri, Poetry London*, *PN Review*, *New Caribbean Poetry, New Poetries IV, The Ringing Ear: Black Poets Lean South* and *The Routledge Companion to Anglophone Caribbean Literature*. His work has been translated into Spanish in the anthology *Poetas del Caribe Ingles*. He was a finalist for the Cave Canem Prize and has received grants and fellowships from Cave Canem, the Arvon Foundation, the Ford Foundation, the Fine Arts Work Center and the University of Birmingham. He teaches at the University of Toronto.

Ishion Hutchinson
Far District
ISBN: 9781845231576; pp. 96, April 2010; £8.99

Far District explores a journey between worlds: the familiar culture of the rural village, which the poet-speaker feels ambivalent towards, and the world of western learning, the "luminous sea of myth" that the writer has felt shut out of because of physical and intellectual poverty. As the poet's journey takes him away from home and into the world of books and learning, there comes a new vision of what "home" might offer – a vision that can be represented through memory and the literary imagination.

Far District is a marvellous book of generous, giving poems. Not only does this collection travel through an abiding language and far-reaching imagery, but it also transports the reader to a complex psychological terrain through a basic honesty and truthfulness. The leap-frogging of borders is executed with an ease that never fails to engage the reader's mind and body. There's a playfulness here that's contagious and, at times, even outrageous in its breathless insinuation through a biting clarity and directness that would have challenged The Great Sparrow. Hutchinson is a young poet who seems to journey wherever his poems take him, and the reader is blessed to accompany him.

Yusef Komunyakaa

Marion Bethel
Bougainvillea Ringplay
ISBN: 9781845230845; pp. 88, July 2009; £7.99

These poems are sensual in the most literal sense – the poems are about the senses, the smell of vanilla and sex, the sound of waves – radio, voices, sea; the taste of crab soup; the texture of hurricane wind, and the chaos of colours bombarding the eye. Bahamian poetry is being defined in the work of Marion Bethel.

Kwame Dawes
Back of Mount Peace
ISBN: 9781845231248; pp. 96, December 2009; £8.99

A retired fisherman encounters a naked, bloodied and traumatised woman standing at the cross-roads. He offers comfort and takes her in. She cannot tell him anything about herself. The only clues are the signs that she has once worn a wedding ring, has a butterfly tattoo and red nail polish on her toes. In the absence of memory, he names her Esther. So begins a remarkable sequence of poems that explores many dimensions of liminality. *Back of Mount Peace* explores the space between body and mind, making Esther's halting discovery of her self through her body, which like a tree bears its indelible history, work both as moving narrative device and a deeply sensual reminder of the physicality of existence.

Jacqueline Bishop
Snapshots from Istanbul
ISBN: 9781845231149; pp. 80, April 2009; £7.99

Framed by poems that explore the lives of the exiled Roman poet Ovid, and the journeying painter Gaugin, Bishop, already between Jamaica and the USA, locates her own explorations of where home might be. This is tested in a sequence of sensuous poems about a doomed relationship in Istanbul, touching in its honesty and, though vivid in its portrayal of otherness, highly aware that the poems' true subject is the uprooted self.

All Peepal Tree titles are available from the website
www.peepaltreepress.com
with a money back guarantee, secure credit card ordering
and fast delivery throughout the world at cost or less.

Contact us at:
Peepal Tree Press, 17 King's Avenue, Leeds LS6 1QS, UK
Tel: +44 (0) 113 2451703 E-mail: contact@peepaltreepress.com